The *Art of* Bagging

The Art of
Bagging

Joshua
GOTTLIEB-MILLER

CONDUIT BOOKS
& EPHEMERA

ISBN: 978-1-7336020-9-9

Published by Conduit Books & Ephemera
788 Osceola Avenue
Saint Paul, Minnesota 55105
www.conduit.org

Book design by Scott Bruno/b graphic design

Distributed by Small Press Distribution
www.spdbooks.org

Cover images: Big John statue, Metropolis, Illinois; photo by
Debra Jane Seltzer, RoadsideArchitecture.com. Grocery ads,
photo by William Andrus. Shopping cart, Shutterstock.

CONTENTS

for Lauren *and* Owen

13:25—

[Do you think you would go out of your way to see an opera if it was about the grocery store?]

Well I mean, the one I work at in particular, or just *a*—

[A grocery store.]

Okay.

[But sure.]

A...okay, I mean, you know that's not, it's not...it's a fair idea. I would shorten it probably by like two hours, because that's the thing, you'd just say, "Would you want to see an opera about a grocery store?"

—Nigel O'Shea (co-worker, Trader Joe's)

The Art of Bagging

It's an art, customer says,
what you do.

Self-conscious of whatever
she thinks I am.

Very aesthetic, I say. Words
mean each thought

inside them. *I'll
admit, it is aesthetically*

appeasing. Ode
to a classic distribution

of light piled on heavy.
Customer doesn't know

what art is, I complain
by the wine. I don't know

what I'm trying to carry.
Maybe it is art,

Whitney says, *if it mystifies
someone for no reason.*

Co-Extrusion

A middleman is suing our chain
for cutting them out and customers
want to know more,
but not about the hundred-foot oven
cleaned of peanut butter
again and again
by someone whose labor
is more repetitive than mine,
and for what?
So you can eat a snack
that explodes
during its manufacture?

Ashley wonders if we also
ever find a word
really weird for no reason,
like *fork,* yesterday
she couldn't get over
how weird *fork* is,
and today it seems okay
on perfunctory inspection.
Whale-road means ocean,
of course, and seahorse,
ship, but the word *kenning*
is only two hundred years
English. It seems strange
that something as simple
as a *fork*
maintains the capacity
to inspire wonder.

I'll never get to clean
that giant oven or walk

the tops of warehouse
rows humbled
by the many aspects
and manifestations
within the word
manufactured,
its limitless forward
movement in space
and instant. *Time,*
long related to *tide,*
coming in and going
out, rising and falling,
willed by the moon's
changing position,
an idea that once
seemed so amazing
we needed words
to explain it
now we don't
think of as invented.

The Brain Trust!

Barry and I have arrived
at a philosophical impasse
re: where to put all these
unattended bags
of pears. *It's the brain trust!*
Boss says, hurrying over,
losing his breath, worried
we are secretly
preparing to ruin
fruit island. Intentionally

naive, there are parts
of this job I keep
from myself: at checkout
this Spanish professor
can't imagine
I know Góngora,
or with an audiologist
share a minute of disbelief
at the ins and outs
of the human ear.

My co-workers
have the most amazing
names—after botanists
and brewers, of
foreign origin or
religious, historicity
inherited and continuous.
I just know *of* Góngora,
really, how hearing
trades volume for clarity.

—And if I knew all of them
I would be able to tell you,
so that you know, which one
is opera singer, printmaker,
cartoonist, DJ, water
engineer, translator,
gamer, addict, three-job dad.

Another poet works here.
Keith's odes have gotten darker.
I wish I knew everyone better.

Emil Alexeivich (Interview)

1:47—

[Emil, you work in a grocery store?]

Yes I do.

[And you are also a translator?]

Yes, I do translate.

[What is…what is translation?]

Translation is bringing one language alive for somebody who doesn't speak that language. So that means to a native language of that person who wants to translate something.

[And I believe you said something in the past about it being like two souls meeting?]

2:20—Yeah, they say…it's actually a Polish proverb, that says, "By gaining another language, you gain another soul." So I think it's like two souls meeting, basically.

[Is that your favorite proverb about translation?]

Well that's first one that comes to my mind.

[And you are also a voice-over artist?]

Well, yep. Voice-over talent they say.

[What's the difference between an artist and a talent?]

I think as an artist you can make up things. Right? You're free to interpret stuff that you know, nobody have to tell you how to do it. But voice-over you have to read a text that is given to you. So there is not a lot of…leeway doing your own art, but just giving your voice to someone else. Borrowing your voice, basically.

[In the grocery store do you feel more like artist or talent?]

In the grocery store it depends—where you have to work. With people or with the product. So you have to be—a bit talented to work with the people I think. To keep your job, you know…[*laughter*] safe.

The Fiction That I Am a Grocery Store Employee

Most of us too old
for skinny-dipping
so Amelia wears a bra
and no panties,
Steve takes off
his glasses, Cindy
a pin from her hair,
and I run in
where the water's
so cold. Old soda
machine's sickly-sweet
glow, river twisted
along the road,
nude as a hand
with a missing
wedding ring, Cindy
says she'd prefer dying
to insignificance, as if
the two are *necessarily*
different. Steve
does a dead man's float
and stars he cannot see
speed above him.
I thought if just one
of them loved my writing
I'd be happy,
then one did
and was that enough?
Doesn't G-d know
a purpose for illusion
is to convince us of the truth
through mistaken evidence?
Just once I'd like to be wrong

about myself and not
have some worse desire.
Cindy and Amelia touch
each other's flaws,
time is not
the opposite
of an echo,
we never started
perfect. I've already divided
what's false from true.
As in a shortcut you
can only use once.

Grocery Store Etiquette

I lose sleep

translating the great drunken poets. All of them
are Li Po. Translating from the Chinese

is like cleaning a grocery store
with a toothbrush.

The wine is cheap
and it adds up. Rain, thunder,
red autumn leaves fall.

My Chinese is bad poetry.

I count my words,
fluff the vestibule, cascade
the bananas. I oracle
bones: bronze and seal.
I official, normal, cursive, running
hand, simplified, divinity.

When I ask, *Would you like
to bag your own groceries?*
I'm not asking if you'd like to save
a tree. I don't blame

the messenger
for shooting the message. I waterfall

the strawberries, I chase
losses, I translate

from the Chinese. I in my whole life
might save one tree.

Which one I don't know.
I won't learn its name.

Luminosity

Ruskin said beautiful art
can only be produced by people
who have beautiful things
about them. He meant nearby.
Glowing fruit stands. Radiant
cans. Synonymless
vegetables. Architect,
build this store over
and over. Cartoon eyes
fill aisles, a child's
sight line. Cereals
pace lower
shelf-heights, brand animals
bait. Baby gorillas, pandas, talking
extinct birds. Walls paint lake
scenes, fields golden, orchards
multiply. Our street of seven years'
mural: family pharmacy
on the other corner, florist,
liquor store, as if from overhead,
beside, animated, caricatured, surviving
our gummy bear drugs and roses.

Studio Time

One problem with being a poet—perhaps the least of a poet's problems—is that a poet can always be "working on something." Other artists are comforted by the restrictions of their media, but I have no canvas, no dividing line, I'm always looking for material.

Walking I advertise my continuous self-scrutiny.

Librarians, set designers, anyone can worry a problem by not thinking about it, until stepping off a bus an equation emerges from the recesses of consciousness—"insight" implying a movement towards—

but for poets walking itself is algorithmic: meaning built in the relationship between an expressed thought and the rhythm of its expression, as in Wordsworth's hill-climbing poems written in Lake District cadences.

Jackson Pollock, instructed by Hans Hofmann to enroll in his school and work from nature replied, *I am nature.*

*

I'm fascinated by the idea of alternative autobiography. Walking as a form of revision. Self-consciousness as a state whose cultivation means I find it odd to continue to learn about myself despite the accompanying discomfort.

*

Why would someone else imagine you were here?

You can be a poet's poet, or an artist's artist, you should be able to be a people person.

Whitney Derendinger (Interview)

[Whitney, you work in a grocery store?]

1:10—Among many other things.

[You're an actor.]

Yes.

[Are you acting right now?]

To a degree...So, yeah, but no more than I think we generally do every day.

[You act in the store?]

Yes, every day.

[Your wife is also a customer. And she also acts and would come into the store and claim that you were pretending to be husband and wife. Would you consider her a regular?]

A regular customer [Yeah—], or a regular wife? Yes, definitely a regular. She's done a new bit now where she pretends that I'm harassing her whenever we're shopping together.

2:28—My wife says that acting is living realistically in unrealistic circumstances. And I *think* acting and theater and art looks to find truth by sometimes putting together things that don't necessarily belong together. I think at the heart of acting there is truth. And I think at the end of the day, when it reaches the audience, it strikes a truth in them. And you can find that by being however fantastical you want.

4:06—

[Whitney what kind of an actor are you?]

Good. That's one of the reasons that brought me to Wisconsin. Because I used to be very pigeonholed as—as the best friend. The person that you like but you—you were never in love with. And so I've really worked to expand what I can bring to the table. So I'm an actor who does comedy and drama and classical work and contemporary and American realism and movement-based work and stage combat—so I am, I'm an actor who—I'm an actor who works.

[And male lead?]

Male lead. Definitely male lead.

Earthquake

Lights go out, mice
from under the freezers
scurry into Peter's story:
Boss joined in. You should have
been there! Hundreds
of tiny heads
caved by every employee
working in concert.
Teamwork. Egalitarian.
Our store stays open
for the lunch crush.
No one might have known,
the mice thrived quietly,
a temporary outage
where there should be a moral.
Peter, our trumpeter,
a California transplant,
sunny and religious,
used to worry he'd be
trampled by stacks
of milk in an earthquake.
A perfectionist.

I Give Our Customers an Exceptional
Experience without Judging Them

Emil speaks Russian
with a shopper
who holds up the line,
who must be grateful
to hear her language.
When she's gone,
Emil wants to know
what I'm writing down.

Three years since I last called myself a grocer
and the dairy box still knows me,
the register remembered
my code. Emil praises my speed,
asks again about the folded paper
now hiding in my pocket.
If he wasn't so busy
as a translator,
he'd be management track.

Plot is information about our futures
we withhold from each other;
I let Emil—tasked with training me—
think I'm just a real quick study.
He beams at product familiarity
I've imported from nine hundred miles away,
back when this was a job
I thought I'd leave behind forever.

Journaling, you're not only recording your day,
but also your thoughts, Emil says,
and we both laugh when I slide
the paper back out of my pocket.

I like Emil: he stands straight
as fresh baguette.
I offer what I've written down
in trade for his animated
Russian exchange.

All shift we stick together,
shopping carts corralled
in the basement parking garage,
he looks around, whispers
that he is not from Russia, exactly,
that he had been with the shopper
negotiating insults
on account of his accent;
he wanted her to know
she wasn't welcome back.

A car snorts,
an elevator winces
behind us,
its slow crawl down
starts up again.
Lean closer, hold tight
the hook that keeps
the carts in line.
I don't want anyone
to overhear
what he's done,
and take offense.
She was wrong, he says,
about my accent.

I'm Always Judging Myself
By What Other People Think I Mean

Christian thinks the guy
who can't keep his hands
to himself is a tragic figure
since he wants people
to like him, which means
Ken wouldn't be so tragic
if he hated everyone
or was just kind of dickish
but kept his hands to himself.
I talk about Ken
behind his back—
I want people to like me—
and swing him slack smiles
when he talks about
customer service.
Ken claims he doesn't understand
the Rolling Stones song "(I Can't
Get No) Satisfaction,"
when it comes on tinny
through the loudspeaker
in the breakroom.
Lunch is almost over,
we don't have time
to interrogate this claim,
check each other's
feigned interest
in what Ken will
and won't get,
whether self-conscious
compensation makes him
more or less believable.

The Fiction That I Can Empathize

I like the idea of a secret life—
coded messages, amoral
vision quests, questions
from the lake when I

take long runs around it—
A romantic
won't deny herself, but aren't people
who they pretend to be?

I'm a sunray
tense in its shine.
It's not appearances
that deceive, it's feelings

in the gap between
hallucination and delusion.
There you go,
pointing your flashlight

behind you into the ghostless
night. Fictions, unlike
truths, can be revised.
Who isn't afraid to commit

thought crime? It's you,
you compartmentalize,
your imagination.
What aren't you thinking?

Bruce Bull Lyon (Interview)

0:18—I'm pretty sure I never said this, but you're the expert.

Bruce reads the poem he is quoted in.

1:29—I hope I didn't botch that too much.

[Bruce, you worked in a grocery store?]

I did.

[Bruce, now you're a customer service associate for a home colon cancer screening test?]

Correct.

[What does that mean?]

It means that I talk to people about their bowel movements all day long. Make sure they collect them correctly. Send them in to us so we can test for colon cancer.

[Do you enjoy this job more than you enjoyed working in the grocery store?]

I—don't know. I enjoy—I enjoyed the people I worked with so much at the grocery store. And that I miss, because it's a different atmosphere. It's a much more—it's much less personal, although you're talking about much more personal subjects. And I just—I missed the people I worked with. Most of them.

2:37—

[Bruce, when I asked you, like, who you are, aside from your job, you mentioned being the minister of sunshine and a prophet of rage—and then you also said that you're uninteresting and a dad and a wiseacre, and you once told me that your life changes when you have a kid. If you were going to square all of those things up into like a ball of a person, who is that person?]

I don't know? Some yahoo, some wiseacre who's a dad who likes to think he's a prophet of rage?

[I think you're a funny guy.]

Yeah, funny or funny?

[I think you're a...I think you're a funny guy.]

Thank you, thank you. That's my goal in life, make people laugh. One of them, at least.

[Is that your wife or kid?]

Pardon?

[Who are you trying to make laugh?]

If I make my wife laugh I...I had a good day. And she laughs easily so I have a lot of good days.

[Could you mention, since this came up somehow in our discussion, of what you look for in a woman?]

[*laughs*] My wife.

Ummm—lot's of things. Interesting. Real. Is this like some new dating thing? It seems like it changed all of a sudden. I'm happily, happily, happily married.

6:54—

[Is there a time in your life you've "gone for 2"?]

Rarely. [*laughs*] I'd like to think I would, though, which might be "going for 2" in its own way.

[I'm wondering, do you think reincarnation only means that the last you returns?]

Good question. I think it's the all of you...I would hope you'd have those memories, and those experiences. Hmmm, I don't know, I've never thought of it that way, which you comes back, because I'm certainly a different person than I was. You know I carry a lot of those same things, but I'm a different person than I was...younger. Probably change when I get older. I never thought about reincarnation, well not that much.

The Fiction in Which My Past Is Behind Me

I no longer tell friends I'm jealous
of the bald eight-year-old
whose poems once seemed meaningful
enough, in light of his dying,
for him to go on daytime television.
Years later, no one's heard of him,
but people bought his books
just before he died.

My girlfriend thinks I have a lot
of deep soul trouble.
She works for a firm soaking up
all the dangerous information in the world.
As in a library. *Glühbirne*
means light bulb in German. Glowing
pear, she says, stepping
out of the shower. "In light of,"
as if the mundane logistics
shaping our continued assembly
of knowledge isn't just staying alive,
which, with enough distance, can't keep
its beauty to itself.

Oh, is the weather feeling me up?
she asks, reaching for a towel.

I am trying to devote myself
to something inside me
that is also above me.
No one asks what the whale thought
of Jonah using its blubber
for light and warmth. Sparks
at the bottom

of a cosmic inventory
in which he'd been
dutifully filed. A trick
to keep the fire so small
even that mythical fish giant,
born of a vengeful and caring G-d,
wouldn't notice.

Planograms

Boss was a boss,
owned his own
sandwich shop.
On my hands
and knees sticking a broom
under shelves of candy:
*Never thought this
is what you'd be doing
with your college degree,
did you?* Boss asks,
but I did,
you told me at the interview.

Boss was a limo
driver, technical
writer, sommelier.
Co-workers watch for you
to look away, kissing
as they change shifts,
sleeping in their cars
on break, forgetting
why we are here.

Military police.
The rival you're dating
who shops in our store;
your children, their expected
athletic successes;
the transfer
you've angled for
once they're in college...
Dallas. For the Cowboys.

Boss moved his family
here, Boss worked
his way up. Boss
is up. I want to know all that
about you, and I do,
co-workers tell me
to. I stare—

you trained
to be a teacher,
composer, draftsman;
directed a play once
—past garish Hawaiian-shirted
corporate pride, rare
unbuttoned neck
giving that WOW
customer experience.

Our morning huddle
by the emergency exit,
a few pitiful piles of dry goods
loiter against the last register,
outnumbered. You point
to the front door,
If you don't want to be here,
you should go.
We've three hours
unloaded the morning truck,
stocking and spacing out
and now of course no one leaves,
which would have been the weight
to give your ultimatum value—

to say a moment is given meaning
by what comes after, not before
—or if not resolution
then its absence does not explain
the nodding heads of crew members
who have understood
in themselves
an identification
with you, Boss,
attainable only via feelings
we'd all (I thought) past disqualified.

And then we're free to go.
Smile! you say, trying to smile.

A Storeroom Is a Moral Universe

because it provides answers
to questions we don't ask. The robbers,

for instance, keep putting
customers in the refrigerator,

there are constantly
more customers coming in

so I have to put more food
on the table—I know I told you this already,

but how are you good today? I'm sorry.
How are you, today, good? I say

to the robbers. I haven't been outside
in years but the windows are large, the light

is good, and I'm not getting skin cancer
from all my time on register. I'll be on register

tomorrow if I don't die in my sleep. I ask
my customers about the weather. I can see

it's sunny out, but people appreciate
being told their observations

matter. Like a workplace romance,
health and safety regulations require

I not get shot chasing the robbers
in the parking lot, wash my hands

to the grindstone, break all the rules that don't care.
I am an empty shelf when I carry nothing.

Sometimes when they're bagging food
or stocking merchandise

I tell my co-workers to do things
they are already going to.

It makes me feel like I'm in control.
Not of their actions, but my own.

Reincarnation

Aphorisms pile up
like opportunity buys:
You have the rest of your life
to get where you need to be
right now, Bruce tells me.
There's no timeline on your life,
he adds. A customer rewinds,
keep taking it easy, somehow
means something more
than to scan
at the pace
I'd set myself she'd
happily accustomed
to, while we shot
the shit like it deserved
its target heart.

An honest person makes
honest mistakes, Boss

lies. Heather asks the juice,
Who will teach me
to love what I'm doing?
And why do I have to learn?

Keith whispers
by the trash, *Remember*
when we worked here?

Shoppers promise,
I could never do
what you do. Do you
understand beneath me?

My belief in reincarnation relies
on this newly dead customer
kicking the soul out
of me or you, but most likely
I mean, when I mean me,
and I do, I believe I will
continue to change
in ways I can't prevent...
to be fair, I've thought
about this before,
and no longer know now
what I was thinking then.

I'm Not a Muse, He Says, There's No Reason

Once I tried to learn everything I could about bananas.

"Sales records show bananas/with Pantone color 13-0858/(otherwise known as Vibrant Yellow) are less likely to sell/than bananas with Pantone color/12-0752 (also called Buttercup),/which is one grade warmer,/visually, and seems to imply/a riper, fresher fruit./Companies like Dole/analyzed the sales effects/of all varieties of color,/plant their crops under/conditions most ideal/to creating the right color."

Eric, touching up our banana abstract (banana island, banana summary, banana habitat), reads poetry when he isn't working seven days a week here and delivering pizzas because he needs to *keep his hands busy.* Eric wouldn't mind being *a monk or a glass overbrimming,* he'd told me, spilling his drink at the bar post night shift, before the band—men who write dairy and frozen and dried fruit—came back on. A gentle guy Boss whispers about, I tell Eric he'll be in this poem: *But I have nothing interesting to say.*

The bananas need stickers to tell us what they are.

I see the city's elegant poet laureate press an avocado close enough to touch Eric, who'd asked me, months before, if I'd read all her books. In seconds I'm introducing them, by the time I've turned back from one to the other, Eric's gone.

(Months later, when I tell him I'm interviewing co-workers, Eric tells me he doesn't have a phone, he doesn't have time, and he doesn't know what I'm after—)

Peter Adam (Interview)

[Peter, you worked in a grocery store?]

1:18—I did, yes. I worked in Trader Joe's for ten years of my life.

[And you're a musician?]

I am a musician, yes. I play trumpet and do it semi-professionally. Well, I guess professionally is the right word. I get paid for it, so I guess that means I'm a professional, right?

[*(chuckles)* I mean, as best a professional can be, right?]

[*chuckles*] Right.

[Can you tell me what's the difference between selling trumpets and milk?]

You have to work a lot harder. People don't need trumpets to live, but milk is somewhat important to survive. Or at least some kind of food. So food sells itself, but trumpets don't do that, for sure.

[I mean, I suppose we could get into a long metaphorical discussion about what it means to need something to live.]

Well that's absolutely true. I mean I might need the trumpet to live, but you know, in the end, probably not.

3:12—It's interesting, what we—you know—doing what I do, and the way that I, not justify, but the way I look at what I do is I am giving the gift of music to people. You know, what our store specializes in is lessons and renting like instruments for school band programs, which is exactly what...how I started.

5:05—My teacher in grad school always talked about the relationship that fishermen have with the sea versus people who just go out on a boat or sail recreationally. People—they both love the ocean, but the person who fishes for a living understands the ocean so much better then, and has a deeper love, but also a fear and a respect for the ocean than somebody who just sails on the weekend or whatever or just does it infrequently. Never, doesn't have—it doesn't exist for them. There's a...not a love-hate, but a respect I guess there, for it. I guess as a professional musician that's how you come to realize what music is, I think.

8:40—The people I really like, my favorite customers are the ones who come in and have been playing for a while and they're looking for their first like *good* instrument. And that's the people that I...that's the customers that I like most because I can find the instrument that can turn them into the next you know...the next great trumpet player, the next great saxophone player, the next great clarinet player [*baby crying in background*], you know that one instrument could propel them on their way to greatness if...if the right things happen. So that's kind of fun to think about as well.

14:10—You know, it's funny, I was thinking about this, before, when I knew we were going to be talking and stuff and I was like, you know, that part of my life, not to sound dismissive or whatever, but it's just like so...it seems so long ago, it's not that long ago, you know, it's like four or five years, but like, I don't know. I guess it was, I guess I've just kind of *put it away*. Do you know what I mean? And I...you know, I think about things every once in a while, like every time I go to Trader Joe's out here I bag my own groceries just because [*interviewer laughs*] it frustrates me when other people do it.

[Yeah, me too.]

But yeah, it's so cliché but that's...that Trader Joe's feels like a lifetime away, you know like it just seems so, so far.

[Do you mean in general? Not just...Maryland,
I mean, cause you had moved.]

Well I mean there's that too, but I mean, I'd worked out of...I worked at Trader Joe's in California, too. And I still see people that—you know—I still see people that I worked with. It's like, oh yeah, you know, I have to kind of remind myself when I go there that I used to do this. Like, I know what's going on here, I—you know—but, yeah, it just seems so, so long ago. I feel this inevitable...that you're going to feel like a different person, but I feel like such a different person.

25:30—*Oh* yeah...I can't believe you didn't bring up what the mice are all about.

[I mean please just jump in if...if you want to tell the story
of the mice.]

So Trader Joe's, in Silver Spring, Maryland, during the winter would have a mice infestation. And it would manifest itself in...you know, finding droppings all over the place, under the shelves especially, and it escalated to the point where customers were seeing mice scurrying across the floor. So I guess we finally decided that this needed to be dealt with because there was too many complaints. And they were even in the milk box, do you remember that? They were in the milk box. Like the coldest place, or one of the coldest places in the store. They were hanging out in the milk box. I couldn't believe that. So anyways, so one night—

[Did you see them shelving any milk?]

Yeah—one night they tore a bunch of—they put all of the product in grocery carts and tore a bunch of shelving down and then found out that they weren't under the shelves, they were actually underneath the freezers, in the freezer aisle, and so—we moved—we moved a freezer, you know, like an upright freezer unit, and there was just this whole...and I mean just hundreds of mice. It looked like the floor was moving with mice. And here are all of these—there's this—there's a bunch of Trader Joe's employees, and this exterminator. And he's like—we're all like well what are you gonna do?—and he's like "kill 'em." So we were literally like crushing their heads under our boots and then like vacuuming them up with like a Shop-Vac and it was the most horrifying thing. It was just hundreds of dead mice vacuumed up into this thing. And then we didn't have a mice problem anymore. Like, just—just no mice left. It was—it was pretty incredible. So yeah, yep. That's...that's the mice story at Silver Spring Trader Joe's. Hopefully it's not, it never was again.

Isn't It the Ghost That's Haunted and Not His Dead-End Workplace?

I'm tired of writing about myself.
It's like anthropomorphizing
a fictional character.
A waterfall.

Our grocery store
confuses, flitting
between genres
of combined absurdly
lists of days
with plots inside
each dazed cashier,
Boss and stockgirl.

Smile! You work here! A shopper grins
up at handsome Christian—
our daily representative in Craigslist's
Missed Connections—
gently hugging lugs of frozen
on his hand-truck.

If this is the same day
Caroline fluffs flowers,
Barry balances pears, holds
them with his eyes,
they fall, he starts
again, synchronized,
he just happens
to work here.

If this is the same day
Christian complains
about the rude remark,
Caroline how the shopper
sauntered past,
Barry how she sang.

Beauty's Workflow

I'm quitting to write alone
in the woods until
my money runs out.

Limp up front
to let Boss know
I'm not coming back.

*Pain is eighty percent
mental,* Boss says. It hurts
too much to nod.

What's Japanese
for continual improvement
that ruins your ambitions?

Kaizen, Boss says,
it's a made-up word—
but it's not, just popular with people

who know what it means
and think that's what it is.
I'm quitting.

I'll quit today.
Dawn pre-thaw commute,
lake ice shines desolate

and I impute moral character
to its buy-in:
every day the lake's

a little more itself freezing
deeper to its core.
A lake doesn't need

to want
to be consumed
by years

it's going through,
interrupted by:
Not everyone's improving.

Because We Sit on a Corner We Are a Corner Store

Impossible to spoil a landscape:
Though I am ignorant how, I say,
I'll see what I can do.

A grocery store is full
of expectations subtly
bruising, turned over
in lonely divided aisles.
You forget I'm looking for you,

but I won't let you get away.
We are shopping
for a new supplier
for your peace of mind,
I say, quoting Boss
verbatim on our product's
unfortunate cross-contamination
with verboten substances.

You guys own it, you say,
you care.

For years struggle
to discard
this lovely moment.

Lennea Rylander (Interview)

1:27—

[Lennea, you work in a grocery store?]

I do.

[Lennea, you are also someone who works, well, doesn't *work*, you lead groups for your church, and teach yoga classes—and captain frisbee teams—and you're interested in studying mental health.]

Yep. Yeah.

[Is there like a word for who you are?]

Well that's a good question. I...I don't know.

[Like, I call myself a poet, which is obnoxious, but Whitney calls himself an actor, and Emil calls himself a translator. If you were gonna tell someone, "Hi, I'm Lennea," what would you say?]

It's funny because I actually kind of like that in itself. Like "I am Lennea." Because I don't like labels, or like putting different definitions on myself. I like the fact that—I like to connect people and bring people together and—I feel like I have a lot of interests and things that I'm pursuing in my life, but I don't feel like there's one thing that, I don't know, like defines who I am. I think for a long time I did have that label, like, "Oh I'm a student," like I went to the UW-Madison, and "I'm studying economics, and maybe I'll be an economist one day." But I think ever since I graduated it's kind of been this just open space where...I don't know. Maybe I'm a grocer when I'm at Trader Joe's, but other than that, I like to just keep it open.

[You like working in a grocery store.]

I do. Yeah.

[I imagine, that's because you like people.]

I do like people, yeah. [*laughs*]

5:23—

[How have you referenced the grocery store in other yoga classes?]

So I like to start a lot of my yoga classes with different meditations and one of the ones that I really like to do is called a loving kindness, or a meta-meditation, where basically you're saying like a prayer or a thought towards yourself, loving kindness toward yourself, and then sending it out towards other people. And you start with yourself, and then you start with a person that you're really closely connected to, and then you start to expand your circle, so you'll move on to a person that you're just an acquaintance with, maybe then a person that you have maybe some animosity towards, and then someone you really have extreme hatred towards. So like widening your circles, and sending them loving kindness. *So* when it gets to the acquaintance part I have a lot of people from the grocery store who come to the class, and then a lot of people who shop at the grocery store and so I'll just kind of bring it up as "and now bring to mind someone who maybe you interact with on a daily basis, but you're not closely connected to, maybe it's your local grocery store cashier, or maybe it's someone who comes through your line if you work at the grocery store," so, there's an example for you.

[Is there a reason that you, when you're working in a grocery store, might start working on that meditation? Start meditating?]

44

I mean I think so. I think that you're closely interacting with people on a day-to-day basis, some of them you see pretty regularly, and you see things in their lives that other people might not notice, even like their family or their friends. I mean there are people who come in the shop and you see them buy like five bottles of wine a day, and so maybe you're kind of keyed into the fact that maybe they're struggling with like an alcohol addiction or...yeah, there's like different things that you see about people's lives based on like the groceries that they buy and your interactions with them. So I think that, I don't know being mindful of your connection with them, and practicing loving kindness is a way to kind of just like...foster those feelings towards them and, yeah, foster a deeper connection when you actually do interact with them.

The Fiction That I Am an Artist

Yesterday I realized I had
changed my life,
now I want to know how
I came to that conclusion.
Married. I have a son.
Iceland? Ireland? Israel?
We could have gone.
How different is that
from looking in the mirror
and wanting to resemble
what you remembered?
Come stare at me,
as I do, and think you must
change your life, as I thought
before it was mine.

Yellow sundown sky a brief strip
between dark gorging clouds
and rain through layers of trees
reaching out their thorny fingers.
Remind myself not to take beauty
for granted, but in the dark
I hear my own limp and think
someone's trailing me.

No one escapes
their own imagination.
The leaves changed overnight
when my son was born.
I am walking on them now.
The energy isn't
in me, it's in the peak
between trees

and trail stored up
in the space
I passed through.
Gathered, it reappeared
when I stopped
to look back.

Studio Time

Co-workers, shoppers, Boss, our friends, neighbors, exes, everyone
thinks we'd make a decent reality show, a better ensemble sitcom.
Something on in the background while you do the at-home equivalent
of coming to the grocery store.

Everything we do is art given the right voice-over.

When the door opens, just a little bit, it doesn't open all the way, you've
got to push. The door's not open, you have to push anyway.

In my "being discovered fantasy," I am not on my phone at the mall, my
face turned just so; I am not writing a letter to the radio show re: the
episode on a highly promising student who forsakes college until the
reporter—previously the student's teacher—goes through her check-
out line by accident. I am not a featured attraction, busking with a
typewriter by the wine.

Near every day I spend one work hour wearing a wine-cork lei, intimate
our store's pleasant inner monologue. No facing product, fixing signs,
passing out samples. Allowed to answer shoppers' questions, but
required to assume you have no questions to solicit.

Caroline Renwick (Interview)

7:00—

[Caroline, you work in a grocery store?]

I do. Trader Joe's.

[And I asked how you would want to be identified and you said, "That's a really hard question, I don't know what I would say" and then you started talking about...the store. You said, "I've worked there ten years," you know, "is this all I am" and various questions about you...you know, what it means to identify yourself. And I'm curious, do you think of yourself, first and foremost, as a grocery store cashier?]

Uh, no, I would have to say that is what I do...it's what pays the bills, although it is more than that for me. It is—because I identify—identify myself in part as a retailer, and always have been, you know it was my first job out of college, I was in this executive training program and for years since then have worked in a retailer—in retail, I think of myself as a retailer—someone who enjoys every aspect of it, from dealing with the customers to merchandising to selling and all that goes into it.

8:52—We—the company has tried to create a very—a small town feeling, where you do know your neighbor, and I think they're...and we are very successful at doing that.

10:00—I may use more words than I need to at times, but I enjoy creating just a really fun atmosphere for the customers. You know, whether it's a single older gentleman coming in who may not have spoken to many people that day, or a mom with four, five children who's you know having a hard time getting through 'til dinnertime. And it's just...fun to see what I can do to make their days seem a little bit better.

12:32—It sounds kind of trite, but knowing that I'm making a difference in their lives is better...but it also makes me feel, you know kind of important in a way. I know I'm working for a great company and representing a good company, but also...I don't know, it just feeds me, being there and a part of that feeds me and gives me the energy. Which you know makes it possible to get through an eight-hour day.

> [You...you must have bad...like, some bad interactions with the store though, *right?* It almost sounds like...I mean hearing you tell it sounds like you're working in a—in a (*interviewee laughs*)—I don't know, some magical—(*Disneyworld—*) kingdom. *Yes,* it sounds like you're working at *Disneyworld.*]

Yeah and it's not like that. I mean, there—sure there are going to be times—maybe not every day, but every other day, where someone can come in and they're just grumpy and they don't have anything good to say and...you know you try and be on your best behavior all the time, but I've been known to roll my eyes [*laughs*] and I've been known to think—[That's it—] I've been known to let people really get under my skin and I'll go and say to one of the managers, you know, "I can't believe what that lady just said," but...I don't know as time goes by I think it's easier to...to handle the less than happy people who come in. Because...I mean, in a perfect world I'd put myself in their shoes and maybe they were having a bad day, maybe they're sick, maybe they lost their job or lost their house and if I was in that position, you know it would be difficult to keep your negative feelings to yourself. So *not every day* is rosy and not every manager is always perfect either, neither—nor are we [*interviewer laughs*]. Nor—[*interviewee laughs*] nor are the crew members, but it's—I think it's a place where you can be human and—you kind of have to be. You certainly can't be a robot and work there, but they let you be yourself and you know that's important.

> [Is there like...is there a single really great or really awful

interaction that jumps out at you when you're thinking about the kind of really human interactions you've had with people?]

The only one that comes to mind is, you know, people who are very particular and are *very* demanding as to how I should do my job. And—and that's understandable, they are the consumer and I'm there to serve them—but also, I do take pride in my work and that sounds *maybe a little strange* because in many people's minds being a stock worker or a cashier at a grocery store isn't...you know, isn't the best thing I could be doing, but *I am*—doing something that I enjoy, whether they—whether they think so or not.

16:25—

[Could you tell me a little bit about being a religious person, or how you define that?]

It's funny I don't...I think other people see me as a religious person, more than I see that myself, I think. And I understand that religion—being a religious person is not—is not going to church every Sunday, it's you know how we live our lives and how we treat our fellow person, and treating that person the way God would want us to treat them. Whether that person is going to treat you the same way or not. And just knowing... one phrase that typically comes to mind is, "There but for the grace of God go I." You know, it's—I am just a hair away from being—in the same footsteps as my fellow human beings, whether it's cold or hungry or homeless and so it's...you know, up to us on a daily basis to look for every opportunity we can to help *those* who are struggling or needy and knowing that we don't often *see* who those people are. That you know someone could come in and be having...look like they're having a great day, and be all happy and cheerful, but really be suffering or maybe just have lost a parent or lost an animal or be sick, and...so that's religion for me. The time will come when I get back to going to church regularly

[*laughs*], I think, but it's knowing that there is—I think you know a
heaven or somewhere beyond this world. Or else I think that would
be very depressing. I don't know, it's just how I—how I live my life
mostly. Again there are days when I'm feeling selfish and needy
and you know like other folks out there, like myself, and it's hard to
remember everybody else.

> [I mean I'm...I'm curious because you had mentioned that you
> recently had...had gone through the losses of a parent and an
> animal, and you just mentioned— (Yeah—) just now that you
> don't know necessarily how other people are suffering, that they
> have just lost a parent or an animal, do you— (Yeah—) do you
> think that—]

I mean there are, go ahead—

> [No no no, you go ahead.]

Well I just—I'm one who lives my life on my sleeve. And everybody
knows that, that's—you know if something's bothering me, kind of
everybody knows about it, I'm not someone who keeps things inside.
And so, certainly, when I lost my dad this last year, well, everyone knew
it because I took time off, but they allowed me to be who I was, but there
are other people who come past me every day in my line as I'm ringing
up their groceries and—something horrible may have happened—God
forbid, you know maybe not but—you know I see trite little comments
on some of these little social media things, so you know just understand
that things happen in people's lives and they're not always going to
be you know—you're not always gonna know it. So if we can err on
the side of being more joyful or understanding then that's just going
to help out our fellow person. Just to give them *a little bit* of you know
happiness if things are going badly for them. And just knowing, just
being empathetic to you know sadness they might have. That they

might not feel that losing their...cat might be significant to me so they might not tell me about it, but I would understand, so...there's just a lot of stuff going on in people's lives, I don't think it's a real easy world that we live in these days. *So.* But there are also things to be grateful for, so if I can do that too, that's...that can be of some goodness I hope.

The Fiction That I Couldn't Do Anything Else

Carrie was scared a drug dealer
would stab her with meth,
get her hooked just like that;
she was sorry she couldn't
drop me off in Philadelphia
after all, to visit my girlfriend.
Later, Carrie accused me
of writing her into a parable
as a fictional character
and killing her,
and wrote a story
where my girlfriend
was Aphrodite,
sleeping with everyone.

In the well-known fantasy comic
by the famously talented author,
a failed novelist summons
Calliope through dark magic,
imprisons her,
more dark magic, and then
rapes her until he is inspired
to finish his book. Calliope, in this wish,
is a beautiful young myth,
not an old woman you dare not touch.

Most understand it's not the muse
but the writer's friends,
acquaintances and enemies who are used
in the creation of stories.
Once transformed
the writer can move on.

The Romantics

J.S. Mill at sixteen
ripping his clothes off
to write genius memos,
pedantic philosophy
at twelve in dead
languages he'd learned
years before
with the ease
of an overworked boy.

Me a lot older, a bit
obsessive re: neatness,
otherwise pleasantly,
relentlessly ungenius:
I leave the register
its math without
barely containing
a contradictory energy,
offer junk wisdom,
lose no part of me
to prodigy.

I'm jealous of Mill—
perhaps alone in my jealousy—
not for his talent
and vision so deeply felt,
but that he loved poetry
without ulterior motive:
Mill recovered himself
after his nervous breakdown
by reading the Romantics.
He was heroically literate.

Mill went to the graves
of Keats and Shelley
just before the idea
to write *On Liberty*
was visited on him.
"We must cram into it
as much as possible
of which we wish
not to leave unsaid,"
Mill wrote,
before continuing
on to Sicily
and the Greek island
of Corfu,
where he thought
he might settle,
Florence and Avignon
where his wife
was buried
before *On Liberty*
could be published.

Bags break most easily
by their handles.
Fruit spoils
from its softest spot.
Think back to a time
your feelings could be shared
by all human beings.
When did you last
take a moment
alone, privately
confess yourself?

Grocers Debate the Apocalypse for Its Effect on Backstock

Lady (nice lady) wants me to know
Jesus works the night shift.

Hide her brochure
in my back pocket. Like a ritual

I shut my mouth. I don't like to be reduced,
even to something bigger than me.

Osmosis

Outside the seasons show
a damning lack of revulsion
for time's continuous error.
"Shock," I am disappointed
to realize, the trees manufacture
from a deep logic of insignificant
corrections revealed,
kinks in the supply chain.
Cold sneaks up
on old maples,
autumn afternoons,
while I articulate "Frozen
Harvest Vegetable Mélange"—
its packaging burnt orange, faded
yellow and green—and
packed down, I
cover it with itself,

our latest shipment:
bright cold bags
shine emerald and gold.
I like to imagine dusk descending
even on the warehouse our truck left
with as much insistence.

> *Did you find everything*
> *you were looking for?*
> *How's your day going*
> *so far?*

Along ordinate and ordinary anthologies
of days thinking "Frozen Harvest
Vegetable Mélange"...

Why did I ask, "so far?"
What could 'everything'
possibly mean?

silence spilling like
milk, unedited endless ellipses,
running tally and total, sum
of some constant distances.

Have I seen you in my line before?
Do you live around here? Do you
need a record of this exchange?

Barry Kita (Interview)

4:00—

[And before the grocery store you worked at, I believe, the Department of Mines and Minerals? As it was then called. Is that correct?]

I worked in a mining consultant office in Tokyo, for ten years.

[Oh wow I had that...well, not totally wrong, but [*laughs*] somewhat wrong.]

4:54—

[Could you tell me of all the jobs you worked, which one is the most...stimulating?]

Oh the mining consultant job was most stimulating. Our company made—helped make government—projects with foreign countries so I was in the marketing department and I would go out to a foreign country and meet their department of mines chiefs, also like the foreign investment chief and we would talk about making a project together and that was a lot of fun for me.

[That is an incredibly fun sounding job.]

21:06—Oh you mean *find myself*?

[Sure, find yourself, define yourself—]

Oh *define* myself, ah, let me see. Well, I'm always interested in trying new things. Lately I've been metal detecting, with Kittle. You remember him at the store?

[Uh, remind me.]

Billy Kittle, he used to [Oh yes, yes—] uh-huh, work at the store. So he's been teaching me how to metal detect and he's taught me *a lot*. And so I either go with him or solo. I look for—an old church or old school, or places that I think haven't been detected. And I look for old coins and—I've been doing this for the past two years. It's really addicting. I feel like I should go out every day for an hour, just to practice. It's kind of like fishing, because you look for a spot you think that something's there, and you try different things to see if you can get something. So, and you also have to be patient. So I've been doing that for a while. You know, let's see what else—

[Can I ask, I don't think I've ever heard someone describe having to practice metal detecting. Is that—]

Well, what I mean by practicing is...okay, you see a spot and you think, "oh, this ground hasn't been touched and there's high potential for finding an old coin." That's what I mean by practicing. Having an eye to see a good spot. To pick a good spot.

[Are you constantly just paying attention as you're walking around, as you're driving around, just looking for good spots?]

Yeah, exactly. It's amazing, what it does to you. So when I'm driving, I'm looking around and I see "Oh, hey, there's a nice hill. *Maybe,* long time ago, the Civil War soldiers camped there." You know, that's what I'm thinking. Or, I look at an old church and I say, "Oh, the ground looks like it hasn't been moved. I know people that go to church always have coins in their pockets, oh I bet you that'd be a good place, they probably lost some coins there." Or I go, I look at an abandoned house, or old school house and I say to myself "Oh you know, people had money, little kids had money at school, oh that might have fell out of their pocket." Things like that. That's what I think about.

[And then?]

Oh, and then I test my hypothesis and I go and I—go detecting there, and—first of all, I look along the sidewalk, right next to the sidewalk, that's a real good place to find money. All right? And at an abandoned church I always go along the sidewalk and I always go right by the gardens. Usually I find something. And then by the parking lot, edge of the parking lot, that's a good spot. And I just go to the easy, easy spot first, and then I try to detect in like rectangles to make sure that I covered the whole property.

[Well that's great.]

Uh-huh. So, I go with Kittle and we just drive around and when we see an *empty lot,* or *old church,* or something that looks interesting I always stop. Try our luck.

[You know, before I interrupted you, there were a couple others you were thinking about sharing. Was there something else you wanted to share?]

Oh no, I don't think so.

A Pleasant Good Happy Experience

Once a shopper confessed, *The sun*
really brightened my day.
Next in line, the next after her,
I invoked it
like a mantra for weeks.
We are encouraged
to feel help means
what you'd want it to.
Monotony requires effort. Non-effort
is a kind of effort, Lennea
tells herself while I pull
hidden cans of baked beans
into the light, to be seen and held,
I'm paid to imagine.
I feel sorry for sun-guy
he came through my queue
and not cloudless Lennea's.
My beard is friendlier than I am,
but my special skill
is I'll wring anything
from anyone: I rung up
Sunshine's words
until a shopper complained
I'd said the same
to someone in front of him,
and then I wanted to steal his regret
I had nothing new
for the brief shock of time
I'd contribute to his purchase.
I'm thinking big picture,
Angie tells herself while I holster
my lucky green box cutter, carry
half a case of baked beans to the go-back

flat cart, and if I think I'm above all this
it's because I think we all are,
but Angie and Lennea know it
whereas I just think it.
"Whereas," I look up and down "grocery,"
I don't know how an aisle scores
the name "grocery,"
or why I convince myself
I have to make that information mine.
The Buddha says if you meet the Buddha
on the road, kill the Buddha,
but when my father was a child,
his mind looked like a filing cabinet,
and though I am a poet
inclined to believe the world is a text
we are writing, I often wonder
what's happened to the hard drive
of my mind when each morning
I load slower and slower.

Metaphorical death by flash flood,
by spider bite and sniper's sights,
by accidental landscape and broke bridge
and endless sinking city
in the poems of my youth.
I want to steal all of it, the Buddha
and my father and every outlandish death
I could look up to
if I make every hour count.
Thinner ice makes more sound,
disasters bore quietly ahead.

Most of This Job Is Case Recognition

Scare quotes
on the register; Angie notices
when she says "yes," to the "amount,"
she's performing rhetoric
on herself. (At night
the registers dream of codes
we enter to use them.)
It's like you're being an anthropologist
of your own experience, Lennea tells her,
tender, ringing her up.
Brandon races by,
back after eight months
of injured reserve. *Give it a week,*

I whisper. End of day,
employees shop, David, dancing
to the Muzak, listening in—
Someone make an employee all-star team,
he shouts—writes his HABA order (soap,
toothpaste, toilet paper) longhand.
Boss asks Brandon,
Isn't this the greatest job in the world?
I can't believe I get paid to do this.
Brandon nods.
I get to do this all day, David shouts
again. (Spins).

I impulse buy some chocolate,
like I've been planning all shift.
Once Boss told me he tried to leave:
I felt a real connection with the ocean,
but his house wouldn't sell.

Years like canvas
tougher than a napkin?

I don't really have any idea
what Boss does,
turns the corner, picks up
a fallen can, he is talking
again and I'm trying to follow
the words he's saying
while making sure they mean
the same things
I think they do.

A Full Shelf Also Hides Its Shame

Boss calls me *Zen master.*
I'm not paying attention.
Turn off the part of my brain
that never got a reward?
Be Pavlovian, Boss says,
not the scientist. There's a clock
on the wall if I look to my left.
Don't turn my head.
Kyle speaks softly, *The managers
are the experiment.*
We're just the wheel they spin.
I try to know myself
by not thinking anything.

*

In the back room
flatten boxes
for the baler.
On the floor
face over
ghost stock.
I'm unashamed,
by what I'm not sure.

*

Proud and lonely
cashiers, interchangeable
as clenched teeth.
*Awareness is the opposite
of thinking,* Marty insists.
*Boredom is only beautiful
when it's a form of pain.*

I wince. Are you a feature
or a cause?
Can you shift from scenery
to moral self-instruction?
Before each checkout
a clip strip of waterfall
greeting cards hangs
the same figure
at bottom looking
up, gravity
obscured by
every higher card.
Understanding comes from looking
at the single representation
we can see all of.
Realize this
for a moment,
completely present.
Take an hour
to write these lines
beneath my grocery list
in seconds stolen
between shoppers—
what are you not
striving for today?

*

I look inside myself: It's me
all the way down.
Then through. It was
as if discovering this
made it true.

Nimi Ehr (Interview)

3:28—

[Nimi, you worked in a grocery store?]

Yes I did.

[You are a scientist? You work in a lab?]

Mmm—I'm a part-time scientist. I work in the lab when I need to.

[What do you do?]

I'm basically trying to sell technology that halfway exists. [*laughs*] We're creating something new. So we're trying to create technology and find people to buy it, simultaneously. So—

[What's the technology do?]

It recovers phosphorous from wastewater, and phosphorous is very valuable as a fertilizer, but it's hazardous in water because it causes algae blooms and that chokes out all the fish and other living things, so we're helping prevent that phosphorous from getting into water-ways, and extracting it as a fertilizer so...farmers can actually apply it right where they need it, so that it doesn't go everywhere.

[You're protecting the food supply?]

Yes, yep, mmhmm. Protecting the waterways and our food supply.

[I wonder that...the title of the poem is "Bouquet."]

Mmhmm.

[I wonder about the connection between the flowers and the grocery store and the work that you are trying to do.]

I do *tend* to like plants. [*laughs*] And other living things [*interviewer laughs*] so there's certainly a connection there.

[So you didn't hate working in a grocery store, then?]

No, I never hated working in the grocery store.

8:02—

[But I wonder: you can see how you inspired this poem. And you can see how you *were quoted* in the other poem. Which poem do you prefer?]

I think I preferred the other one, because I recognize more people in it. I guess I'm just thrown off by Nabokov, I have no idea who that is.

[He's an author.]

Okay, well I figured as much, Mr. Poetry.

[*Lolita*?]

No. What?—

[*Lolita*!]

I'm sorry, I like science! [*laughter*] I don't read books for fun, I read them for information.

8:45—

Well, I did enjoy our produce encyclopedia. But yeah, I guess that's not great literature. It's just an encyclopedia.

> [I wonder if you're the only person to ever enjoy a produce encyclopedia?]

C'mon. I can't be the only one.

10:42—

> [Did you have any kind of relationship with the food itself, or did it just not matter?]

God I love spoils. I loved when we had cookie spoils. [*laughs*]

And, yeah, I definitely had a...I don't know, I cared about the food, I paid attention to where it came from, because that was always interesting, to see when things would switch from like Mexico to Guatemala to Peru, just to see and imagine where they were coming from.

> [Country of origin?]

Yeah, country of origin, totally. See what was in it, where it was cane sugar or beet sugar was kind of interesting, and if it was beet sugar it wouldn't specify that it was. Yeah, the subtleties, yeah, mattered.

The Same Simultaneous

I still can't remember
the name of the customer
Boss told us don't worry about,
sweet old long-time regular
we wouldn't ever see again,
children moving her
to Boston to be closer
to them and live
in a home and
yes, she won't be dead,
not yet; I never
would have thought about that.
One day she returned,
more forgetful and obstinate,
I realized that's who
Boss meant.

A blizzard is laying its first layer
of tomorrow down.
Boss convinced we need
to want to be here.
We had to shovel our way in.
Now I'm out of uniform, no
box cutter, no name tag,
picking up lazy provisions.

Pushing by me, her empty cart
like a walker, more layers
than body, she motions
me over. Time restates,
clarifies, as in a single
frozen frame. She thanks me.
We were *here for her,* she says.

Nigel O'Shea (Interview)

2:28—

[Does it seem at all strange to you that you, having worked
in a grocery store, also in radio operations have worked on
food reviews?]

No, it seems to be kind of like where my path has led. Because I spent a
lot of time in my life—working with food, but I'm also for the last six years
have been working—trying to develop a career in radio, so of course it
makes a lot of *sense* that I would create a *radio feature about food.*

[But you came to radio through music?]

Correct.

[Do you feel like music and food was then combined in your
move to radio, or are they just like weirdly parts of your life?]

3:16—I would definitely say that I live my life through my ears. And
so—and you know am a musician. And so it was just kind of an easy
fit and once I was introduced to the world I found it to be really—like
kind of second nature, like I was really comfortable in the environment,
and I understood it, I understood listening to my own voice through a
microphone, you know? I understood like transitions and how time had
to run and it just...it just all made sense to me. And I think a big part of
that is, you know, training in music.

[Do you feel like in the grocery store you're...listening for music?]

3:57—I think in the grocery store I'm inundated with music, actually.
Outside of my own choice.

[Well aside from like Muzak?]

Sure.

[Yeah.]

I—unfortunately I would prefer a quiet grocery store—and I think the Muzak—maybe like you're trying to lead me to, it—it destroys any ambient noise or noise that you might appreciate in a quieter space.

[And you would appreciate that in a quieter space?]

Yeah for sure. I mean I think for a lot of people, I guess shoppers or consumers, it's really disconcerting to go into you know a public place without piped music, you know I think it makes them uncomfortable and retailers know that so that's why they provide that soundtrack, but me personally, because I have to work in that environment for eight hours, would appreciate just ambient sound. And the sound of people's voices.

Hard Work Makes Work Hard

When I was four I'd fill
a Flintstones car
with toy mower
and flowers, plastic bat
and tricycle, building blocks
and GI Joes and coloring
books, the lines untouched...
the years later I would
compare myself to Rauschenberg
in the supermarket,
with his shopping cart.
Rauschenberg said "the artist's job
is to be a witness to his time
in history," but he meant "erasing
a drawing by de Kooning."

My father's hand was shaking
when he asked me what it was doing,
surprised I didn't know why
he was pointing it out, but it took
someone else—a man older
than my father—who
almost couldn't hand me
his single gallon of milk
to make me silent
for the register's hour,
which was, like all hours,
made up of thirty-six hundred seconds,
of which this exchange
was the only one
I remember.

"Idea" is a comforting word.
I made my structures for the joy
of knocking them down;
my parents only kept pictures
of the structures standing.
"Revelation." "Concealment."
I tell people bananas
are going extinct,
but everyone already knows that.

Small Talk

In the refrigerator
behind the dairy shelves
a task worker
took off his gloves

to write on the wall, "kill
me now." Only he phrased it,
"I should kill myself."
Bored at the register

by the multitudes it
contains, I don't small talk
a shopper challenged
speaking English. I won't

put pressure on her short time
staring at the screen
to be sure I don't overcharge her.
Was it our nihilist Sam's

joke suicide note? Like the box
of expensive wine with markings
from our inventory months before
crossed out—under the obscured

numbers, "Put me out of my misery"—
the only wine we can't sell.
How's your day going? I ask,
finished bagging for Ms. Quiet,

before the receipt's filed
with her groceries. *My husband's*

in the hospital, she says. *It's a long drive*
so I'm staying at a motel. I'm not sure

how long. Gone. Barely
wish her husband well.
Sam seems upset I hate him.
Franciscan Magnificat;

a new uncle, I'll buy a bottle
for the bris, scourge
my hands, I don't want
the baby to get me sick.

Marty Gross (Interview)

2:20—

[Marty, you work in a grocery store?]

I do.

[Marty, I asked how you would define yourself, and you said...you didn't want to define yourself.]

Yes.

[(*laughs*) If you could define yourself, how would you?]

Well Emil called me an artist. I wouldn't go that far. I would say I'm closer to a performer.

[I've noticed that you often change your *look*. You've got like this aesthetics of your appearance—]

Right—

[You know the...beard, the facial hair in general, the mustache area (*interviewee laughs*), the hair, I always love your hair, you're always doing something different with your hair.]

So—

[The glasses are beautiful.]

Thank you. Thank you. I try to just do whatever it is that I'm going to do and let other people if they so choose—define themselves—define me for myself, I guess. You know, it's not up to me.

Staring at the Lake with My Wife after My Morning Shift

What happened? Lauren asked.
I'd started at this branch
a little over a year before,
spent three months revising my expectations
downward until the holidays. Since then it was a marriage
of convenience, me and the grocery store.

She should have chosen the other cashier, I said,
quiet. We lived in a one-bedroom on Lake Monona,
downhill from the Capitol. When it had been too cold
to snow we would wake up to a horizon of glittering ice,
marvel how we had learned to live so well
with so little. Now summer lay light on the lake.

She asked for plastic bags. I'd already bagged everything
in paper, I guess I took too long so she clarified
she used them for her dogs. "As a chew toy?"
...I don't know, because of the way she said it?
The subtlety with which she refused to articulate
stooping to pick up dog poop?

Lauren sat silent, looking out at the sailors,
drinking her one cup of coffee,
the one she'd saved until I got home.
You know I don't think that was even it.
She told me she used "our" bags
because they were biodegradable. "They aren't,"
I corrected her. "A manager told me so," she said,
so I explained that manager was wrong.

I pulled the yellow complaint from my pocket.
I didn't mention I'd been too late to my register
for one truly gorgeous sunrise, through abundant

street-facing windows its reflection
illuminating competing stores' displays,
while we were unloading the truck driven
all night to our isthmus, how we worked
through three dawns: twilight, the rays the sun
shot over the horizon, sun breaking the plane.
I didn't want to admit
I'd pitied this ten a.m. shopper,
she didn't know what she'd missed.
I could have just given her plastic bags,
more than she asked for,
and in a thousand years they'd disappear.

Remediation

Mark Bradford became Home Depot's
Mark Bradford when he bought paper
and paint supplies from stores
he painted. Brendan O'Connell used to work
from photographs taken in secret,
now Walmart gives him a cherry picker
for superstores. It is tempting
to slide from one painting to another,
from exteriors to interiors,
to go deeper and deeper into the coincidence
that turns the machine into art.
At Employee Appreciation Night
(no drinking allowed)
Boss convinces Ashley
music causes sales—salsa
music for chips, Sinatra for spaghetti—
but sales always change, only
in one sense improve; I'd like to say
I don't give a shit, but Ashley gets chills
at work for weeks when a song comes on
she knows. I too have confused
"interior" with "entire," and a person
with my day. Boss has hired
a band of stockers and cashiers;
we scream giddily along to lyrics of hatchets
catching in undead brains, workers scrubbing
floors all their lives, meteors wiping out
unnamed mid-sized state capital university towns.
One song mentions an employee by name.
Boss—*Team leader,* he tells us,
when we call him that—says,
This will never be spoken of again.
But he waits until the end.

We clean up, make our store safe
for Muzak. Co-workers
who gyrated together, bodies free
as empty soda cans, now fill shopping carts
with unopened bags of chips, slowly wheel them
to front-load empty shelves. "Hollywood facing."
Nigel catches me double-checking
triple-stacked yogurts,
and shakes his head.
I like the phrase "shift work."
I like to sing along to songs
about our crew. I eat
apples and oranges we stock,
shoppers tell me
they can't live without.
Even yogurts think
they're someone's muse.
Make no mistake, Nigel tells me,
we got paid.
We didn't just do it
out of the goodness of our hearts.
Someone pumps The Clash
over store speakers, "Lost
in the Supermarket,"
bright lights blaring, young men
when they sang it.

Botany

Scan me: my flowered uniform
pierced by name tag enough.
Autonomic, like a blush,
or as in a painting
meaning myself first
and only then confirming
—pre-conceived—notions
I might have. My world is
neither new nor baffling nor begs
to be reinterpreted: A catalogue

of shelf-stable advertisements
of inner beauty, elements
of such a diverse nature
to throw one in my cart
is to hallucinate
a healthy weekend.
The rare off day I'm here
anyway: The objects remain
the same but I am materialized
anew against a new background,
studying fruit I just bought. I belong.

Adam Thein (Interview)

[Adam, you worked in a grocery store?]

2:40—Yep.

[And you're a musician?]

Yep, that's right.

[What's the difference between your ambitions as a musician and your ambitions as an employee?]

I feel like my ambitions as a musician are more closely related to who I am and how I identify myself and my ambitions as an employee at a grocery store are more of a means to an end. It's just a way to get a paycheck I guess.

4:15—As you are promoted and you feel like there's more and more of an expectation of you always being positive and happy and kind of...you almost feel a responsibility to the people that you work with and who work for you that you need to kind of lift their spirits and kind of make everybody feel okay that we're all working at a grocery store together.

6:30—You almost have to kind of decide that you are giving up your ambitions in other parts of your life in order to devote so much of yourself to a retail job like that I think. And there were definitely people—like, my direct supervisor, he really liked working at the grocery store somehow and had kind of—he always talked about the time when he kind of had a similar experience where he had been there for several years and thought this is just kind of just what I'm doing until...the thing I want to be doing comes along, and then finally he said one day he realized I'm happy here, I'm able to make a living here and I think that's kind of a...shift in his thinking where he realized he wanted to be there, as a career. And I think that kind of gave him more energy to be there and want to be there and convince other people that they want to be there. I guess for me, that never really...hadn't happened yet, and I'd worked for the grocery store for four years at that point, so—

10:06—And when those opportunities happened to come along—I started as a cashier and was making like $10 an hour when I started and it was an opportunity to make an extra $3 an hour for something like that—for a supervisor job, it was kind of a no-brainer at the time. When I *was* promoted it did feel all of a sudden invigorating, like "Oh this is a good company to work for, I was able to get a better paying job here." That sort of thing. But that kind of wears off over time...four, five, six months down the road the newness of it kind of wears out.

12:57—It was definitely a decision that, I don't know, I'm not really sure why I wanted to take on more responsibility. I think it's easy [*interviewer laughs*]—it's easy to see the raise and see it as an opportunity to, you know, when you're making $10 an hour, making $13 an hour suddenly seems like a lot more money. Like "Oh I've been making it on this amount of money, $3 more an hour, you know that's great, I can like go out to eat this week or"—

[*It is,* it's a lot more money—]

Yeah—but yeah, I don't think it's always the case—and I think it varies from retail location, like from place to place. I have...an acquaintance from my hometown who has actually been pretty excited about an opportunity with like a convenience store chain and I've been trying to convince him not to do that. Like right now he works in health care— I'm not exactly sure what his role is but he makes decent money—he says the assistant manager positions at these convenience stores are like a really strong salary, even better than I think some of the managers at the grocery store where I worked were...what they were making. But I'm trying to convince him not to maybe give up—like the money seems good but it really—working a retail job can really be all-consuming especially as a manager I think, so—

15:57—It's kind of like a...group delusion like you're part of this giant company chain store, but you have to—in order for everyone in the store to justify feeling comfortable with that you have to—kind of have your own identity, I mean I can even remember having meetings where we talked about that—Packers games or whatever on the radio and...it was kind of—it was easier to swallow I guess, working there.

18:07—I think the word *family* was thrown around a lot, too. Like you're grocery family or whatever. And to some level at least it did...it felt that way, at least to me at the time. Saw a lot of the same people, you know.

20:07—Kind of been going through another transition coming here to Eugene where we live now and I don't really actively make as much music as I used to so it's becoming kind of less of a part of who I am in certain ways. So yeah, I don't know, that's a great thing for me to... reflect on. I'm not sure. At least for my art-making and—or what, I don't know, my aspirations have changed so much just from a couple of years wanting—you know, I've always thought '*Oh* I'm a...I'm a musician and I'm going to be a musician for my entire life' and I've kind of reached a point where I'm not really creatively active right now and—I've gone through a few phases like this before where it's kind of slowed down a lot and then picked back up, but—I don't know, this feels different. It feels like a crossroads though. What I want to accomplish...do I want to accomplish something with my music or is it realistic any longer? I don't know, I feel like I've reached an age, I'm 29 now but—kind of looking ahead, like—should I go back to school? I don't know, maybe I'm having a bit of an identity crisis because I've, at least the last decade I've definitely felt like I was a musician kind of trapped with my work, and now I feel like I'm...you know, my work isn't satisfying and my creative part of my life has kind of—dwindled, so now I'm, yeah I spoke about video games as an escape, I guess it's kind of also just a distraction, or like a holding pattern maybe, a way to put off making any real decisions about my life, so—it's kind of where I'm at right now.

22:17—Yeah, I think that's a big part of it. I think being in a band as opposed to making music as a solo artist definitely adds a lot more structure. You're...you know, kind of relying on each other more. And pushing each other. I think that definitely would be a big part of why I've kind of lapsed off with my creative...parts of my life. Because there's no one else with expectations or pushing me to do it, you know, it's kind of all on me now. I bet, or I can guess that maybe you have a similar experience in your writing? It's kind of down to you to decide what to make and when to make it and how—and how much time and effort to put into it so I guess I've found out that I—am a little bit lacking in that self-motivation for my solo creative process. Hopefully I—

[No no no, what were you going to say?]

I was just going to say that I...kind of have this hope that, you know, I'll meet somebody eventually that is also interested in making similar music to me and we'll kick it off and have another band happen, but you know, the older I get the less likely I feel like I can *do that,* so I don't know, I don't really know what's next.

Value Added

Our value proposition: low price,
decent quality, for when just good enough
has been your standard so long
you come to believe in it as life philosophy.

Walter de Maria, in his essay "Meaningless Work,"
which glided along behind his performances
moving boxes back and forth—
no, the contents of one box to another,
wooden blocks—
says meaningless work can make you sweat
if you do it long enough.
Like ordinary work.
Flying a kite, laying train tracks, listening to *Peter and the Wolf*,
all provide too much pleasure to be meaningless.

Camouflaged and poisonous,
I repeat the phrase
    conventional bananas
at least once a day.

Our Greeting Cards

quote Tennyson and Dickinson
and Blake:
"Hope is the thing!"
"No bird soars too high
if he soars with his own wings!"

I love the idea of the memorable.
The innocence of the masterpiece.
"The fox provides for himself,
but G-d provides for the lion."

In fact, to be fully understood,
"meaningless work should be done alone
or else it becomes entertainment for others
and the reaction or lack of reaction of the art lover
to the meaningless work cannot be honestly felt."

Bodhisattvas, bodhisattvas,
HQ made some changes,
so Boss joked computers
track our work ethic
to reward appropriate discount
when we clock out.
Good luck, Dickie says,
once we're alone
in the breakroom.
I work hard
and with a bad attitude.

Many Strata of Feelings and Memories,
Even Working Here Every Day

The young man posing
his gorgeous wife frowned
when I said I didn't remember him.
What appears unique
of course becomes beautiful,
as in a plant survey.
I wonder if he saw me when he came in,
his hands aching as he walked by
Mike throwing frozen.
We rode the bus together in second grade.
You and Zach sat at the back
and bullied me until the stop at Wire
and Normandy. His wife
suddenly recognized me. That's where
Zach and I would have gotten off.
Did I offer sincere apologies
for actions I still can't recall?

His wife touched his ear
and he touched her hand
touching his ear...
a growing tree root splits a stone,
perhaps what is beautiful seems
a reward for your attention?

Botanist doesn't want to see the forest
for one specific species of plant
he needs. A cliff hugs a pine relic,
as a wildflower to variety,
each uncompromised
by a singular definition of beauty.
Years later, I remember so little

about him again, as I remembered
so little about him then.
Horticulture requires jealousy.
I envy the clarity in which he fixed
me. He left shaking
his head. Grasp at the purity
of this moment, in my utter horror
of self-knowledge
dodged, though I try to be impressed
at all times, as a botanist would,
not by waterfalls and cliffs,
but a wildflower
close enough to pick.

Keith Leonard (Interview)

2:08—

[Keith, you worked in a grocery store?]

I did. [*laughs*] I worked with...I worked with you, Josh.

[And Keith, you are a poet?]

Yeah. I try to be. [*interviewer laughs*]

[Go on.]

No I mean and—working at a grocery store as a poet is...a really interesting experience because—you're around people all the time, which sometimes is not always the case when you're writing.

13:33—

[Have you always been a teacher?]

Mmm—I've always been a student. [*laughter*] *So* I mean—I taught—I got an undergraduate degree in secondary education, and I taught for a year in Massachusetts, and then I went off to grad school where I taught you know some intro college courses and whatnot. Yeah, and then... wound up with this job, which I really like.

[But I mean you're—I mean you're not just working a job? Like you—we've talked, you're there watching basketball games, you're meeting with parents, you said that you're *planting an orchard* with your students?]

Yeah. It's an incredible thing, like I—working in this high school, it's this private high school in—Columbus, Ohio, and they're...there's a lot of really amazing school spirit. Kids actually enjoy being there it seems, or at least don't seem to take for granted the fact that it's this school that really cares about their education. Like they...they're all about teachers just teaching what they're best at, right, and not just teaching according to standards or...anything like that. So—I got to—I'm teaching a course next spring that I'm planning right now, where we're gonna, with the lower school, with anywhere from kindergarteners to sixth graders we're gonna be *planting* this giant garden and eventually some fruit trees and then a lot of the food that—grows will go to food deserts in Columbus. So, for people that don't really have access to a lot of fresh food. But it's great, we're going to learn about it, too—we're going to learn how to—garden through literature, so we're going to actually read some—some great literature on gardening, and then actually put that into practice. So I'm pretty excited about the class.

45:31—...But I know just from my own like experience of—of *writing*, when I'm working—because I've worked as a landscaper and a caddy, and—a lot of other—worked as a deputy shellfish constable, once, which is a weird fact, but—it was all, like a lot of physical jobs, right? And I've found that when I...when I work physical jobs I write so much more. Even though my—I'm bodily exhausted—my mind is constantly on poetry and like memorizing poems and its got a lot of drive to like—I don't know, to just—for my mind to be someplace else as my body is going through this physical exertion. So for me that's where—like right now I'm trying to memorize poems, but—I can't because I'm constantly in my mind, thinking of—for teaching, right? And I don't have a very much of a—physical life right now. I've got a nice little dad paunch going on [*interviewer laughs*], basically—

49:08—

[I think the question I have about a lot of these poems is: is this
accurate, is this honest, does this tell the truth? But even when we
were there we weren't always thinking about what was happening,
we were trying to be somewhere else...we were hoping to get
somewhere else, we were thinking about where that could be,
and maybe even trying to create that, right?]

Mmm.

[Did you ever...did you ever feel that way? Like there were things
that maybe you—you kind of—you said "I have to do this" and
then you—you tried to?]

How do you mean? You mean...you mean in art?

[Well in art, shit, in life.]

There are things like where you—like you set a goal, how you're talking
about like—like dreaming essentially and then making it happen? Is
that what you're saying? Yeah, I mean I feel like that's sort of been my...
my life story until now.

As Long As There Are No Other Questions, This Has Been a Great Day

Today Boss moves goods onto shelves
and assists customers
in organizing these materials
for future putting away
in cabinets and refrigerators,
remembers to me
bad dreams of being
an employee. He says
he'd put the closed sign up,
but customers kept
coming to his register,
and I have the same nightmare,
the customers trying
to do my job,
only nothing
they scan rings up
so I check them out again
as the line does what it will,
all circles being alike.
I'm the only cashier here.
Boss is *calling it a day.*
He's not wrong!
Has he reached his moment
of singular necessity?
Does he look inside himself
for the manifestation
of his hidden essence?
Is it boss after boss
all the way down?

I'd like to say this life
is what I'd imagined, beauty

as symmetry
between expectations
and their fulfillment, fire
from ash. Career, family,
friends; sounds nice
I would have said. My state tree
is a stump, flower
the first one up.
Introspection? I see through
myself. Relax,
turn my back, the life
I didn't imagine sneaks out,
unwanted, only consequences,
but all of them.

Studio Time

It's harder to pretend to be working than to actually work. This is true of much in life, but not poetry.

Nimi's worked up the courage to ask our former combat medic for a quick concussion check he doesn't need to perform. *Welcome to permanent brain damage!* PJ says—what her concussion literally meant—she hesitates, so I joke PJ and I are figments of her mind.

I can't tell if Nimi believes me and in her second hesitation I start to worry. Déjà vu, but not mine?

Erased brushes and buckets, the snow on our truck fallen a state over, the cold clear and long with passing through.

Point of Sale

Take a moment, muse
everyman, adjunct

grocer, actor rehearsing
patience. Did you study books?

Wouldn't you rather be
idly scribbling? How goes

your inner
spit-shine?

Let your hopes
begin inspiring

"under bleak fluorescent light,
a two-note aria."

Christian Dewey (Interview)

11:40—I don't...I mean personally I don't think a poem has any obligation to Ken at all.

[Can you tell me a little more about that?]

Well, this poem seems like...I mean, it's—there's—it feels like the speaker is working something out, that the narrator is working something out that's personal, and Ken is a *catalyst* for that process and—and—[*sighs*] I don't know, I mean...does any poem have any obligation to anything, I guess?

14:30—

[Christian, you worked in a grocery store?]

Yes.

[And you are a geochemist?]

Yeah.

[Can you tell me why chemistry is more interesting than retail?]

14:49—[*laughs*] *Oh man—Well*—so, my work at least is more challenging than—the work I do now as a geochemist is more—more challenging and intellectually stimulating than the work I did when I was working in a grocery store. But I—I don't know, I mean it—there were plenty of interesting things about working in a grocery store, too. And sometimes I miss...the ways in which working in a grocery store was interesting.

But I don't know, the thing that I—the reason—the reason that the work I'm doing now is a better fit for me is that—I feel like I need the intellectual stimulation and the challenge of—or the challenge that I find in my work, which I wasn't finding as a worker in a grocery store.

[You know Barry always told me that he preferred retail to the work that he was doing. He was working as an engineer I believe for the Department of Mines and Minerals before he worked at a grocery store. And he always said like it was boring and I just couldn't fathom it. I guess that's just—what's at the center of my question, which is that you don't—you don't find your research boring.]

No. Not always, I mean sometimes I do. There's a lot of drudgery in what I do, too. But for the most part I'm interested in what I do and I find it motivating. Yeah.

18:17—That's true, yeah. Well I think that's part of it, yeah. I think the questions are—well, they should be questions that haven't been asked before. But, for me—what's motivating to me is that the questions are difficult to answer, and they're not straightforward, they're not simple questions, and—they're difficult to answer rigorously and in a way that is—that minimizes uncertainty. The challenge is—both developing the question in a way that's interesting, and then also developing a process for—providing evidence for your answer. And—*usually*—it's the process of developing evidence that's really, really challenging. It's really hard to...say, figure out how uranium is bound to an iron oxide. That takes a lot of work. And it—the answer might be simple in the end, or it might appear to be simple, but the work involved in—finding evidence and data that can...provide an answer with the least amount of uncertainty is really challenging. And that challenge that I like—maybe that challenge is partly a function of asking the question—that's new, or that hasn't been answered. I guess if there were...or it had been answered, then people would know how to answer it. And it wouldn't maybe be as challenging to answer.

21:28—...A good pressure? Yeah, I mean it's a pressure I enjoy. I guess I am detail-oriented and I—you know I do like—I like understanding the details and I like knowing something with as little uncertainty as possible, and you know one thing I've learned in a year and a half of a PhD are that there are *not* as many things as I thought that I know with very little uncertainty. I know some things with little—with very little uncertainty, but there's—that's a small list. That's a small list. [Sure.] The part that...the goal of research, or at least the research I do, is to know something with as little uncertainty as possible. And there's always going to be uncertainty. You know there's always going to be some way to—interpret the evidence which isn't in line with the—our hypothesis, or the way that we've answered the question, but, the goal is to minimize that uncertainty.

22:43—

[...I don't think I've heard scientists use the word uncertainty as much as I hear you using it now, and I wonder if there's some connection between maybe the way you're using the word uncertainty and the way a poet might use a word like truth or beauty.]

Mmm...hmm...that's interesting.

[I mean when you say uncertainty, ultimately the goal—when you say your goal is reducing uncertainty is it simply to find things that—I mean it's not just to find facts, right? It's to find like really important—or is it just like even basic facts that are so hard to be certain about. I mean what—is there more of a connection there?]

I don't know, there could be. I...yeah I'm talking about more than just basic facts, more than knowing basic facts.

Well you know sometimes when I'm—when I'm say reading a scientific paper, you know I do pay attention to details, and I think about reading a novel or reading a poem or reading something non-scientific, something creative—I like to pay attention to the details and when I'm reading in that context, too, you know when I'm reading a novel I like to—say if I'm reading about a character in—in his bedroom I like to imagine all the details of his bedroom, it doesn't feel—that different really than what I do when I'm thinking about reactions on an oxide surface or something. Still trying to imagine what's going on in that world. What it looks like—

I don't know. I don't know if there's some deeper connection to beauty or truth or *whatever*. Maybe.

25:05—

[What motivates you to do the work you're doing now? The kind of science you're doing now?]

Mmm—that's a complicated—you know the answer to that question is complicated. I mean honestly sometimes I think—I feel like I'm just along for the ride here, you know? It's like—I am still surprised that I'm doing a PhD in science and I'm not quite sure how I got here. [*interviewer laughs*] I think back to nine years ago when I'm—you know I was an undergrad in—studying English and...I would never have guessed that I would ever end up doing a PhD in science at Stanford, but here I am. And I can't quite explain how I'm here or why I'm here, I mean I know I like the challenge, I know I enjoy work that—focuses on details and I have fairly strong analytical skills and I like doing something that I'm good at, but—yeah, sometimes it just feels like I'm along for the ride. And I—I'm intentional about what I do—I...it doesn't always feel like intention and choice are what brought me to this place entirely. Maybe some other—somehow you know—something out of my control helped me get here. I'm not necessarily talking about some *divine* force at all, I'm just—it, you know, sometimes it feels like—I'm moving forward with time and it's taking me somewhere and I just don't have control, complete control over where I'm going. That's not really an answer to your question. [*laughs*]

37:42—You know sometimes I miss it. And I—I'll go to Trader Joe's here in California and—you know a few times—a few times I've gone wearing an old Trader Joe's shirt and some of the crews at—or some people on the crews at these stores here have stopped me and talked to me and knowing—it seems like there's a...there's a connection, that they...*they recognize* that maybe I know where they're coming from or what their work is like, and I don't know. Somehow I—I like that, I like sort of escaping from—from this insulated world of—on Stanford campus you know, among many people who have never worked a blue-collar job or you know had any sort of challenge in their life, any—any professional challenge that wasn't academic.

> [Do you have a...feeling of camaraderie, with the people in the California stores?]

Yeah, I do.

> [You know it's funny because I feel that way sometimes, about the store in Houston, I'll go in, it's just up the street from me, it's like two blocks away and I'll go in and I, if I haven't met someone I'll find some way to slip in the fact that I used to work at Trader Joe's and—and ask them about how their day's going and you know try to have a good interaction with them, bag my own groceries, stuff like that. But I—I mean I don't know, I didn't burn the shirts, but I *know* I gave them away. I know they no longer are in my possession (*interviewee laughs*), because the first time I stopped

working for Trader Joe's I left them...I was living in my parents' house at the time, and I left those shirts there, vowing *never* to come back for them, and when I got a job at the Trader Joe's in Madison my parents like brought the shirts for me like thinking this was a nice thing to do (*interviewee laughs*) and I was like "No this is *horrible*. Why is this happening?" So now those shirts are no longer to be found. I could not tell you what happened to them. (*interviewer laughs*) But you still have them, you still...you wear them to the store every now and again.]

You know I only saved one. I only saved one. And—yeah, I don't know. I—I—sometimes I like feeling connected to that—that life I had.

Moral Physics

One ethic subsumes another
when the grocer feeds his family
by working through a flu
and so infects the town. Morals
too are viral, as in a painting
the way we see is not the way
we understand; the student on a bus
who hits a baby with his backpack
has no one to blame; contrite,
the bomber's father dies
in the care of the military
hospital. One ethic steps aside
when in a movie the vigilante
stabs a mugger and reluctant
takes the unloved bystander
home. Hamlet
misses a good play, attentive
to his uncle, Ophelia dead
already, a character study.
I cover Steve's register
while his wife phones to say
their nephew thinks
he's in Afghanistan; he's got
his gun and two girls and
this is just sinking in, she doesn't
know what to do. *A double-bag,
that would be perfect,* my customer
explains, then *Circles are the strongest
shapes,* she adds, when she sees
her eggs are whole. *But chickens
have hollow bones,* she adds
again. One ethic admits it's not
helping, one insists on its survival

despite a useful negligence towards
the rule of law. In the miracle
of the synagogue, in the animal
kingdom, in flowers by the outdoor
auditorium. Parasites infect snails,
burrow eyeballs, stretching eyestalk
imitation caterpillars, fish they turn red,
floating, ants march to the tops of grass
blades, scroungers attracted to light
shooting their spores towards sunbeams,
birds ingest and propagate, the light scatters,
cows chew and pass. One ethic, anti-
camouflage. One ethic, two directions.
Life is one enormous contradiction: Éluard,
the French rebel whose poem, "Liberty,"
snuck past Vichy censors, assumes the word
and all its valences written in every tactile surface
on the mind of his country, a Communist,
later praised the hanging of a friend
in a Czech purge. In history a bystander appears
free of harm. In a dream I don't
hurt anyone. Your mission on this planet:
wrong only yourself. You have,
and more. Our fantasies involve impossibly
small kindness. One ethic for the many,
the same ethic for the few.
The banality of good. Morality that appears
in the first act must go off by the last.
Shrapnel over bent praying heads, a hole
in the bima, bomb unexploded
in the courtyard. The blanket
for the boy as his parents' house
is searched. A hit and run

that leaves the bicyclist unscathed.
The conversation and she misses the soon
colliding train. Before he leaves, Steve gets his coat
and asks the Boss permission. Caroline says
she'll pray for him, I wish him speed, Boss
tells him he can go. One ethic reveals
another, as in a palimpsest: the first moral
says nothing about the silent law beneath it,
the later train waits quiet on the tracks.

Dialogue

If Rauschenberg says the tire is art,
it's art. It's painted, after all, by him,
and performative, rolling down the aisle
at his friend's funeral.
If Rauschenberg says the tire
is not art, it's correspondence,
sits in museum archives
overlooking books and letters.

It matters if other people see you as an artist, Lindsay explains—
anti-diva, mezzo-soprano—when she won't sing
for us. She's written
her final dairy order I'll unload.
We thought she'd leave
to join a touring company. She dominated
local repertory, wrung herself all craft;
she's moving back home now
management track. *Aren't we always ready*

for the adventure not to begin? Keith asks,
licks goodbye frosting
from a butter knife. He's memorized
twenty poems here, he's ready
to forget them all.
Lindsay's made it half a decade, Keith won't
get a cake, the hour the crew takes turns eating
and begging her to sing.

When a customer buys flowers
I say, *Flowers? For me? Thank you!*
They laugh, and I laugh
and I ask, *why did you laugh?*

Bruce mentions a wine he likes.
What did you do? he jokes.

Before our son was born
I asked Lauren to trade
this isthmus for a country
where we won't take
beauty for granted.
She wouldn't go that far.

An artless passage of time?
What box won't an artist
sink into?
What myths of what's next
won't we leave behind?
The last time I quit
Boss promised to save me

my job. Consider unconvinced:
the downtown art gallery
wedding planner committee,
local news obituary proofers,
politicians I volunteered for,
prison wheelchair delivery
and service. This is my third time
tied to this chain. Once,

returning to my first store, Chef Charlie
(*but he's not a real chef!* my father complained)
asked if I still wrote. He's a poet.
I'd forgotten: stray publications in his youth,
magazines overseas, wayward pieces mentioned
in passing, wistfully. Years before.

So Chef Charlie and I caught up; five minutes.
I won't put him on any pedestals
he didn't want. The day after Lindsay left
I worked her section, no opera
pouring over store speakers.
Keith promises I'll read his poems
when his book comes out.

There is no door the artist lifts
in back of the store to walk
into a bigger story.
This is how most artists live:
We don't make it. Resisting obscurity
in retail jobs, advertising, grant writing,
we don't prize or recognize ourselves except
by unending pursuit of entire lives.
We feel out of place. Forgotten
by others and then ourselves.

I've been in town long enough
to spot poets who shop here
off-campus—flowers, wine,
chocolate?—a line
is starting to form. Oh yes,
I've learned lessons simple
as hard work, turned my life
into an elevator pitch
even I dismiss
for lack of conflict.
Couldn't you remain invisible
in increasing ambition?
I believe I'll never stop writing,
but I'm terrified my struggle
is its own reward.

My wife knows my epiphanies,
cares which ones are interesting.
Unlike the great artists, it's not
an open question if, for most of us,
our shopping lists show
promise. Doodles on letters
to friends. Books I've read.
It won't be a great event
when the records of my life are left
unrestricted to the public.
My wife, after a decade's climb,
labors at an elite museum library;
I run my tongue over her title.
She stopped writing
to focus on her dream job,
friends, our family.
You mean like me,
she says. *What*
are you afraid of?

I Am Often Reminded That I Am Here to Help People

Boss takes his lunch with us, asks how my day is going, like I am a
customer. *Average,* Boss says, about his own, before I can answer.
And then *Average is below average, because I prefer my days above-
average.* This afternoon he'll see me use a milk crate as a ladder, write
me up. (*An injury is paperwork,* Boss reminds.) This will make his day
only more average. Another time, Boss will write: *Being intentionally
confrontational with our customers has a negative impact to our store.*

Forgive my supposed disbelief in self-congratulation, the minor
victories of my sneaky know-it-all heart. I felt as if I was floating when a
shopper asked about my inner employer. I shrank when a shopper said
she was *satisfied just being alive,* but wasn't sure if she was *setting the
bar too low or high.*

Did you want your receipt? I asked.

Now I can tell you nothing else about that day. Like many days, perhaps
I'd woken to lush winter-blue sky all night shivering, ice in the lake,
surrounded by cold landscape. My inner employer and I could tell you
about the stark singular laser eye of the register, its pure verticality—
Whistler's fireworks, Barnett Newman's solitary black lines—I had
wondered then, why do I look down, past warnings in four languages,
and not look every single customer in the eye?

ACKNOWLEDGMENTS & GRATITUDE

There are too many people to properly thank for making this book possible. Thank you to Lauren and Owen, first of all, and always. Thank you also to my mom and dad.

Many thanks to the University of Houston Creative Writing Program, Inprint, and the MacDowell Colony for their generous support.

Thank you to Bob Hicok, William Waltz, and *Conduit* for believing in *The Art of Bagging*. Their generous reading and tireless work is greatly appreciated. Thank you also to cover designer Scott Bruno for finding Big John. The statue is one of a fleet of aging giants guarding an old chain of Mid-America grocery stores. The Big John on my cover is one of the last ones left; since the photo was taken he's lost one of his arms, but he stands tall nevertheless.

My thanks to teachers who have given me guidance and inspiration, especially Lucille Clifton, Kevin Prufer, Martha Serpas, Tony Hoagland, Hayan Charara, Nick Flynn, Roberto Tejada, Ange Mlinko, Jeffrey Coleman, Edgar Silex, J. Kastely, and Sarah Ehlers. Thank you to Carl Lindahl for teaching me folklore.

Special thanks to my readers, especially Niki Herd, Stalina Villarreal, Allison Pitinii Davis, Fritz Ward, Brandon Lamson, Lauren Berry, Glenn Shaheen, Keith Leonard, Becca Wadlinger, Caitlin Plunkett, Adam Vines, and Charlotte Wyatt. Special thanks to the poets I met in Madison: Rosanna Oh, Steel Wagstaff, Ryan Browne, Joshua Kalscheur, and Oliver Baez Bendorf. Thank you to Carolina Hernandez and Kevin Doyle for invaluable help early on.

Thank you to Carrie Ermler—the desk at the Cy Twombly Gallery and the back desk of the Menil Collection provided necessary perspectives as I worked on this book.

Thank you to Sehban Zaidi for help editing film and Adam Thein for help editing audio. Thank you to The Bubbler at Madison Public Library, where the first interviews were filmed, and Digital Media Instructor Nate Clark for his assistance and advice.

Thank you to my interviewees.

Thank you to my co-workers.

*

I am also grateful to the editors of the following publications, where some of these poems first appeared:

Bat City Review: "Grocery Store Engineer"
Birmingham Poetry Review: "The Art of Bagging," "The Romantics," and "A Full Shelf Also Hides Its Shame"
The Brooklyn Rail: "Studio Time"
The Cincinnati Review: "I Am Often Reminded That I Am Here to Help People"
Grist: "The Fiction That I Am a Grocery Store Employee"
The Laurel Review: "Grocery Store Etiquette"
No Infinite: "Point of Sale"
Pank: "A Storeroom Is a Moral Universe"
Pleiades: "Moral Physics"
Radar: "Co-Extrusion"
Rattle: "Staring at the Lake with My Wife After My Morning Shift"
Talking Writing: "Reincarnation" and "Bruce Bull Lyon (Interview)"
The Texas Observer: "Luminosity"
Variant Literature: "Beauty's Workflow"

Thank you to the editors of the following publications, where some of these hybrid and multimedia works first appeared:

Grist: Poem and interview via "Grocery Store Scientist," poem and interview via "Grocery Store Translator," and poem and interview via "Grocery Store Musician"
marrow magazine: Hybrid essay "Grocery Store Performer," includes a re-printing of "A Full Shelf Also Hides Its Shame"
MAYDAY: Hybrid essay "Grocery Store Artist," includes a re-printing of "The Art of Bagging"

ABOUT THE AUTHOR

Joshua Gottlieb-Miller earned his BA from St. Mary's College of
Maryland, and his MFA and PhD from the University of Houston. He
served as Poetry Editor and Digital Nonfiction Editor for *Gulf Coast,* as
well as a Post-Harvey Think Tank Fellow for folklore at Rice University's
Humanities Research Center. He has been awarded fellowships to
MacDowell, the Yiddish Book Center's Tent Writing Conference, and
elsewhere, and while at UH won the Inprint Barthelme Prize in Poetry
and the Inprint Robert J. Sussman Prize. He has published poetry,
nonfiction, hybrid, and multimedia writing. He worked at Trader Joe's
three times: once in Silver Spring, Maryland, and twice in Madison,
Wisconsin. He currently teaches at San Jacinto College and lives in
Houston with his wife and son.

CONDUIT BOOKS
& EPHEMERA

OTHER TITLES FROM CONDUIT BOOKS & EPHEMERA

Thunderbird Inn by Collin Callahan

The Birthday of the Dead by Rachel Abramowitz

The World to Come by David Keplinger

Present Tense Complex by Suphil Lee Park

Sacrificial Metal by Esther Lee

The Miraculous, Sometimes by Meg Shevenock

The Last Note Becomes Its Listener by Jeffrey Morgan

Animul/Flame by Michelle Lewis